Search for a Velvet-Lined Cape

Search for a Velvet-Lined Cape

Poems by Marjorie Manwaring

Mayapple Press 2013

Published by   MAYAPPLE PRESS
                  362 Chestnut Hill Rd.
                  Woodstock, NY 12498
                  www.mayapplepress.com

ISBN 978-1-936419-15-9

ACKNOWLEDGMENTS

Thanks to the editors of the following journals who first published some of the poems in this collection:

5 AM: Disappearing; Ephemeroptera; Joseph, Flying; and Kitchen. *A Sense of Place: The Washington State Geospatial Poetry Anthology* via Google Earth: Trying to Get Across. *Crab Creek Review*: Kiss, You Ask About the Letting Go, and Refusal. *Crab Orchard Review*: Church Camp-out, 1978. *The DMQ Review*: Letter from Zelda and Rejection Letter from Gertrude Stein. *Diner*: Tiger Trick. failbetter.com: Baton, Levitation, and Musée Mécanique. *Fire on Her Tongue: An eBook Anthology of Contemporary Women's Poetry*: Thinking About Someone I Used to Love. *Floating Bridge Review*: As Fast as You Can, Colors, Endangered, We Have All Entered a Nesting Phase, What Ignites, and Restoration. *Four Corners*: The Magician's Lover. *FRAME*: Bill of Health. *Hubbub*: Yellow. *In Posse Review*: The Magician's Mother. *Jack Straw Writers Anthology*, Volume 10: Charm and The Princess And. *Karamu*: None of These Belonging. *Natural Bridge*: Before the Mind (published with a different title). *periphery: a magical realist zine*: Sculptor. *Pilgrimage*: What Rises, What Wanes. *Pontoon: An Anthology of Washington State Poets*: Eskimo Pie and Weekly World News. *Rock & Sling*: After Sunday School and A Quiet. King County Metro Poetry on Buses: Leaving some shell of yourself. *The Seattle Review*: Groundhog Turning Poet. *Sentence*: Reappearing. *shaking like a mountain*: Letter to Mick Jagger from the St. Paul Chapter of the Daughters of Norway. *The Smoking Poet*: Escape Artist and rpm, 1980. *Switched-on Gutenberg*: Greetings from the Dead Poets' Convention. *Swivel*: Company Party.

"Magician's Assistant" and "Treasure" first appeared on the Wenatchee Valley College web page, Mirror Northwest. Cornucopia won the Artsmith 2010 Literary Award and was published on Artsmith's website. Some of the poems in this book appeared in the chapbooks *Magic Word* (Pudding House Publications) and *What to Make of a Diminished Thing* (Dancing Girl Press), and some were reprinted in the following anthologies: *Collecting Life: Poets on Objects Known and Imagined; A Face to Meet the Faces: An Anthology of Contemporary Persona Poetry; Fire on Her Tongue: An eBook Anthology of Contemporary Women's Poetry; New Poets of the American West: An anthology of poets from eleven Western states; Northwest Renaissance Poets at the Kent Canterbury Faire anthology; Jump Start: A Northwest Renaissance Anthology;* and *Northwind Anthology*.

A note on the poem "Disquiet" (page 70): This is a cross-out poem from a page in *The Street of Crocodiles* by Bruno Schulz.

Cover art by John A. Clapp (JClappart.com). Cover design by Judith Kerman. Book designed and typeset by Amee Schmidt with titles in Minion Pro and text in Californian FB. Author photo courtesy of Susan Filkins.

Contents

Part Four: **Now You See It . . .**

Part Five: **Voilà!**

For Mom and Dad—thank you for a room all my own, a shelf full of books, the Hocus Pocus magic kit, and so much more.

Leaving some shell of yourself

covered in sheets, you catch
your bus, pull the cord ten blocks
early, walk into the store that sells magic.

When your boss asks where you've been
you say you wanted to learn

how a thing disappeared comes back
how a velvet-lined cape
feels against skin.

Part One
Bending Spoons

Tiger Trick

So a magician, a mentalist, and a poet walk into a bar. Always the same questions when the other patrons learn their trades: *Do you know how they do that tiger trick in Vegas—Have you ever met The Amazing Kreskin—What kind of poetry do you write?* The magician is reading about the physiology of Houdini's lungs. *Do you know*—he nudges the poet—*that Ginsberg guy had quite a pair too. Practiced reciting his lines face down in the bathtub. No shit—in the tub!* Meanwhile, the mentalist orders drinks telepathically and realizes how tired he has grown of bending spoons and always knowing the punch line. In fact all three are bored with the particular way they exploit the malleable. The magician sometimes wishes he were lyric, but he gets such great results with *voilà! presto, change-o!* and *hocus-pocus.* And the poet, yes, the poet—he keeps trying to saw his words in half, dreams about pulling a sestina out of his hat.

Musée Mécanique

*mechanical-amusement-toy museum in San Francisco, featuring coin-
operated "Laffing Sal," a larger-than-life papier-mâché woman who
laughs hysterically*

Sal's gigantic arms jerk up. Her laughing fit begins.
Harmless! No shocks! A prize every time!
Watch a toothpick Ferris wheel spin and spin.
Are you the captain of your fate?

Harmless! No shocks! A prize every time!
The Mystic Ray tests love appeal.
Are you the captain of your fate?
Hold hand firmly down on plate.

The Mystic Ray tests love appeal.
Modern Vibra-Massage Chair relieves fatigue.
Hold hand firmly down on plate.
Ask the Mummy answers with a shriek.

Modern Vibra-Massage Chair relieves fatigue.
Insert coin, peer in.
Ask the Mummy answers with a shriek.
Reclining addicts heat their pipes in the miniature opium den.

Insert coin, peer in.
Watch a toothpick Ferris wheel spin and spin.
Reclining addicts heat their pipes in the miniature opium den.
Sal's gigantic arms jerk up. Her laughing fit begins.

Letter to Mick Jagger from the St. Paul Chapter of the Daughters of Norway

Dance with us, Mick,
leader of the full lipped
double-joint-hipped man-girls: panted
tight, eyelined,
come-hithering.
Have you guessed
we like a bit of gender-
bending? Bring your fast fingers,
your limber derrière,
Tuesday nights we're here—equipped
with dance floor and liquor
license. We can offer you our hand-
made rosettes and hot-
from-the-oven Julekake.

How excited we'd be
to see you squeezed
between our
agenda items next month:
Lois Giske's slide show
on "buttons and fasteners
of antiquity,"
our yearly
membership drive
at the Cork 'n' Fork.

We're tired
of acting 50-something
and know you
won't hold us to it—
unlike our husbands
who've forgotten we
were Woodstock, free love,
used to want us
to start them up.

Greetings from the Dead Poets' Convention (a Postcard)

Got in on a technicality (my near-death experience counts!). Rooming with H.D. and Anne Sexton. No such thing as a friendly game of Scrabble with those two, and don't even get me started on the "words" we have to allow when E. E. Cummings plays. Keynote speaker is Pessoa—rumor has it he demanded four podiums, time for wardrobe changes, and a look-alike puppet. Last night Keats and Shelley started a fistfight with the Beats (the offending comment went something like "take your romantic iambic head out of your consumptive pale flat ass"). Mother Goose (also admitted on a technicality) broke it up and received a nasty blow to her left eye, but Dr. Williams patched everyone up in no time. Whitman and Rilke have discovered karaoke and there's talk of revolt—dead or no, a person can listen to "American Pie" and "Danke Schoen" only so many times, though with Gertrude Stein and Anonymous egging them on, I think we're in for another night of it. Last evening's martinis were strong and things got a little out of hand: Sylvia P. answering every Trivial Pursuit question with a line from "Daddy"; Emily D. leaping out of Jack Kerouac's lap, letting rip such a string of expletives that even Allen Ginsberg blushed. Not to complain, but I had such expectations—brightest minds engaged in political debate, literary criticism, the chain poem to end all chain poems . . . but I'd better go as I can't miss this—Ezra Pound wearing a lampshade, Neruda and Sappho lip-syncing "Greased Lightning."

Joseph, Flying

Joseph of Cupertino, a priest who had the gift of levitation and ecstatic visions, was eventually investigated by the Inquisition. Though no fault was found with him, he was sent to live in exile. He died in 1663 and was canonized in 1767.

In tonight's dream he relives the first time
lightness consumed him: a summer walk

barefoot through the lemon grove
toward three tall cypresses

adorning the landscape like candles in a cathedral.
Strangeness takes hold,

his heart beating faster.
He feels weak, light in the head.

God and the sun
play tricks with his eyes

so that all he sees is a field of yellow
haloes and he begins to float, up and up,

the backs of his outstretched hands
scraped by cypress's leathery leaves,

scent of the earth and sun-soaked lavender fading.
He hovers near the top of the tallest tree.

His heartbeat slows. He regains normal vision,
sees two grey pigeons

roosting on separate treetops, warbling
and nodding at each other,

ignoring him, just another dull
clumsy bird . . .

Come morning, he might
recall the dream, though he won't

dwell on life as it used to be—before the stern
voice of the bishop: *Your flight*

disturbs us, before he was asked to
exercise restraint.

These days he likes to repeat
a verse from John, the one

in which Lazarus is raised
from the dead, Jesus telling the crowd

Unbind him and let him go.
He and Lazarus shared that once.

Being unbound.

Before the Mind

Before the mind
overexerted itself

on gravity, on proofs,
what habitat for magic—

neurons not so tightly packed,
wiggle room for prophets

potions and gods.
Dreams meant something.

Take Jacob and his ladder.
Take Pharaoh and his corn,

lean ears swallowing up the good.
You believed what you saw

though vision wasn't bound by eyes.
No need to analyze Medusa's writhing head,

reduce her to a queen with dreads
who served her minions psychotropic drugs,

or theorize Midas's Golden Touch
into a meteorological phenomenon of the sun.

Thinking About Someone I Used to Love

It makes me sad because I've never seen such—such beautiful shirts before.
—Daisy Buchanan, from Fitzgerald's The Great Gatsby

Is it overly romantic
to want to see
through *spectacles*, not *glasses*,
to wish the sign
on the door read
oculist instead of
ophthalmologist,
to desire a man
who owns a stack
of long-sleeved dress shirts,
to cradle those linens and silks,
to brush their luxury,
their meticulous weaves
across your lips,
to feel pleasure as you
watch him hold
your favorite—periwinkle
—the one with nearly invisible
pink flecks, imagine
what he's thinking as he slides
each arm into its sleeve,
pops each button
into place, pats down his front
and tucks the hem into pleated
unbelted trousers?
You wonder if he wonders
about words, how they can change
everything, East Egg
to West Egg and back again,
the distance, far and not far,
between the valley of ashes
and this place, where at dusk
the gulls call madly
as the city lights up the sound.
Is it foolish to mourn

the eras of elegance
and danger that have passed
you by and will you
take this chance
at love, a gangster
with a wardrobe full of shirts,
because aren't all men invented,
riffraff still clinging to the bottom
of their shoes, and isn't he a man
who promises, promises, and
won't you choose
to believe him?

Weekly World News

The supermarket tabloid ceased publication in 2007,
but weeklyworldnews.com lives on.

When Bat Boy is finally found—eyes
unfocused, sixth sense rabidly
clicking away—sharing a cave with Elvis
beaten down from a papparrazzi'd afterlife,
waving his soiled rhinestone cape like a soldier's
white flag, when Bigfoot, D. B. Cooper, Hitler's clone
unionize, agree to appear on a crop-circle set
for one ratings-rocking Oprah show . . .
when the world-weary alien refuses to endorse
a presidential hopeful, impregnates
a virgin who's been frozen in an ice block
since the Kennedy administration . . .
we will know this is it, our kitsch Armageddon:
Oh bubble tea rosaries, oh bobble-head
saints, deliver my soul on a spork
to the icon with the biggest two-page spread.

Rejection Letter from Gertrude Stein

Dear Poet Dear Author Dear Someone:

We are pleased very pleased
To regret sir.
Regret to inform you the list for
Talents selected not you dear.
So many many and many
Many talents not you dear.
Received many fine not you.
Thank you extremely fine thank you.
Keep us in mind please keep us.
Please keep
Your submission in mind.
Entries so fine many fine
Winners selected not you.
Not you. Not quite
What we need
At this time not quite.
Keep in mind best of luck next time.
Editors wish you this guideline.
Best of selected regret.
Not chosen you were not able.
We inform our regret.
We reject your receive.
We receive we regret. Inform you we do.
We do as we do.
Today: To do: Don't forget.
Difficult choice we regret.
Space an issue weren't able. Limited
Space unable.
Please
Accept this issue.
Our complimentary
Gift to you.
Letterpressed gift in which you
Do not appear we regret you.
We regret to reject with respect
Please accept. Do

Not not accept
This reject
If you do
If you do
With respect
With respect
We reject you.

Magician's Assistant

The man by my side, patting my collar down, brushing cat fur from my sleeves before my appointment with the magician—he knows, my husband, the importance of these nights and yet still wonders what it is I seek at the magician's house. He knows there's more to it than a rabbit and a hat or a shell game, and tonight his hands will linger on the abrasions—*Yes*, I'll say, *he's still working on the sawing trick, almost got it down* and I don't know when this fantasy grew to such proportions—the magician, the magician's assistant, but this man by my side, he sends me on my way and as I open the door he says, *You forgot something*, hands me my dog-eared paperback on illusion and escape.

Bill of Health

I don't do high-velocity adjustments
says the chiropractor, *you've*
got cobwebs in your heart, says
the massage therapist, *there's*
a curse on your line says the fortune
teller, *but for $25.00 we can change that.*

Part Two
Altered States

Levitation

She enters in darkness
(he forgot to turn on the porch light again), walks in.
Sees him haloed in blue tele-light, eating popcorn in the Barcalounger.
He turns to her. *You look pale—levitation again?*

Yes, sets her keys on top of the TV.

How far up this time? He holds out the bowl, she shakes her head.

Three feet—he's trying some new spells. She smells envy, sits.

Loud chewing. *Tell me what it's like again.*

*The floating—it's almost unnoticeable, like
lying on a really comfortable bed, and—*she hesitates—*there's a sound.*

Hmmm? His jaw pops.

A faint—singing. The butterflies.

Questioning look, slow swallow.

*Butterflies, he keeps them about—wings, cocoons, for potions.
When I go up, they fly alongside. And . . . sing.*

Well, I've never heard of . . . Like birds?

*More like crickets, or frogs. The magician says animals
can sense transformation. But I'm the only one who hears them.*

Eye contact. *You mean he can't?* Chewing stops.

Just me—he says it's part of the altered state.

I was in an altered state once. Big swallow.

She remembers. *Yes.*

No butterflies though.

No, she kneels down next to him, head in his lap, *no butterflies.*

Ephemeroptera

In that time, just a few remained
who asked why each bud of the rockrose
bloomed for just one day,
or why the female mayfly
winged up from lake-bound larval mud
only to die before she'd breathed the sky five minutes—
though not before mating and laying her silver-sac'd eggs
in the waters from which she'd just emerged—
or why the human eye so honors flames
and sunsets, those brief sculptures of orange
and crimson too soon subsumed
by ash or dusk. Or why the art
of grave digging had undergone a renaissance,
the earth perfumed with bodies adolescent, unbloomed.

rpm, 1980

Spinning
     my new

     (shut door)
          (close curtains)

          Cruisin' 45
             (over and over)

         me spinning Smokey
     spinning me

through the thick
     of what drifts

         through bedroom
            window screens—

mothers' *Come home* calls
       August's sprinklered heat.

    I see
       what my vanity

     mirror reflects—
turntable spinning

     knickknacks, figurines
     how my night-

gown clings
     and falls

my hips moving
(this way)

my head tilting
      (that way)

how his voice leaves
me spinning

(shimmering)
        a giant super-

imposed on rows
    (Dutch milkmaid)

    (southern belle)
of purse-lipped storybook dolls.

The Princess And

Because of it, this gift or curse, she's spent most her life an insomniac. To the prospective mother-in-law it's a sign that she'll cater to the prince's every whim, being able, as she is. To perceive as she does. And, being the highly sensitive princess, she will. Attend to. Intuit that. Anticipate everyone's every move. There's no relief for a girl like that. Even one molecule carrying the scent of an unpleasant day oppresses her . . . . Each night she hopes for sleep, tries so hard. To eliminate all wrinkles, rubbing the flat of her hands across mattress pad, bottom sheet, so, yes, a nickel will bounce when dropped. But it doesn't have to be a pea. Or even a pucker of fabric. A loose down feather will press violently against her spine; she'll feel the restlessness of dust living under the bed.

As Fast as You Can

Oh, haughty cutout cooling in the breeze,
think hard before you lift yourself from two
simple dimensions—think before you run!
Even if your leap to cool linoleum
finds your limbs intact, think of the cat, the
dew-soaked grass—you're not the sturdiest stock,
kin of cakes and soft breads who had no dark
raisin eyes, no frosting mouths—had no heads!
No mouths, no longing, no bravado: *You*
can't catch me! Ginger Boy, they can—the truth
is, a plastic spatula released you
to a trickster, a shifty-eyed foxy
world, its hot red hunger, duplicitous
tongue, teeth that snap cookies and dreams in two.

Escape Artist

I'll be a juggler. No,
a swimmer. Manacled

like Houdini. Able to maneuver
my way out of any sort of box

even underwater, even dangling
from a high rise.

Did you know as a boy
he picked up needles with his eyelids?

For my first act I will wire walk across Niagara Falls
—how I love to listen to you oooh and aahhh as I

tiptoe across life's chasms.
Meanwhile. Pssst. Keep your eyes peeled

—I've rigged my balancing pole to turn into a rabbit
after I nail this triple Salchow dismount.

Thank you, thank you, and now
that we've all had a moment

will my sparkling assistant
please draw her sword?

Ladies and gentlemen—I present you with a real live
levitating man. No strings (witness her blade slashing air)

no mirrors! And again, please bear with us as my dear assistant
fetches her theramin, accompanies my departure

with an otherworldly opus . . . . Oh yes,
oh yes, it is quite lovely up here

though I'll miss the one-armed unicyclist's derring-do.
How I revel in this life as a spectacle

even as I become smaller
and smaller to my earthbound audience below.

What's Left

All time is unredeemable.
　　　　　—T. S. Eliot

One gets used to reading the face
of an upside down clock.

Some transposing, quick
thinking. (Never mind

the blood on the living
room wall.)

Tick and tock
the hour is late

—second hand circling,
the future a mad-mouth

with everything to lose.
Suicide, you

silver-toothed demon, keeping exit
at the center of things.

Where Sadness Lives

The mural on the cafe's west wall
—a fantastical underwater scene.
On the left a chorus line of shrimp
wearing top hats, sporting canes
(think Mr. Peanut but pink)
though the last in the line
looks wistful, makes me feel
sad when I look at him
the pang increasing
when Susan tells me
he bears an uncanny likeness
to her great uncle Nicky.
I know you were probably
expecting something real—
a secret life I learned about
only after someone died
or the golden retriever
tied outside the supermarket
and struggling, its legs tangled
in a worn leather leash—
but I seem to see suffering
even in the animated dog
who lives in my computer,
searches for files I've misplaced.
When he digs and scratches
and wags his tail, then looks up at me
so wanting to please
I feel badly for replying "No"
to the question "Did you find
what you were looking for?"
The silver lining: we hold on
to triumph where it can be found—
the homing pigeon named Marty
who broke his wing in a 300-mile race
yet returned to his owner
on foot two weeks later.
The paraplegic veteran
whom the scientists are studying.

They've hooked wires to his brain
so he can turn the television on
and off with just his thoughts.
And so it goes, energy expended,
much of it on the pursuit
of happiness, though it surprised me
at last week's symposium
to hear the physician say that the human act
requiring the most energy is dying.

December Meditation

Yesterday stalks of calla lilies drooped, transformed by frost into
    cranes gathered at the front porch.

Have you noticed how a cat tests one paw before stepping out into
    late-night snow?

On the second Sunday of Advent the bishop becomes St. Nicholas,
    wears a red pointed hat, hands out ginger cookies wrapped in
    cellophane.

'Tis the season to abide bells, and melancholy.

I miss that classroom smell of cut-and-paste, linoleum floors littered
    with glitter, pompons, scraps of felt.

This morning "end-of-the-world man" with his giant inflatable globe
    handed out cartoon tracts in the downtown square.

Pies with sugared crusts cool on the kitchen table overnight.

Inside the cathedral, the midnight procession begins: organ in the loft,
    incense, "O come all ye faithful."

I roam the neighborhood after dark, gazing at the bright star, rows of
    houses trimmed in colored lights.

Colors

For you, blue mother: a corpse
(the boots, the knock, the wail)

and you, green sister: the veil
(the wreath, the stripes, the stars).

Purple brother we give you a heart
(the trumpet, the brave, the spill)

and scarlet father: a hole
to fill, to fill, and to fill.

You Ask About the Letting Go

Yes a softness
       gripped me
a feather-beat
of down
Held me with
   a mother-bird ferocity
      Yes
       (still gripped)
I think I was still
I think I was still a body
     (or something)
      holding on
to skin

What I heard
      before ascent—
your voice
A voice low, muffled
—what we hear
  (a hum)
from within
  from within the womb
  (a heartbeat)
      What I heard
     —assent
        (a voice, low)
to leave
     to leave behind
  earth's peach
  summer's night green

     Night's hum
and wingspan
    feathers filling
    nine-o'clock sky
What I (still)
hear—
humming, you
  (scent of cherries)
  (scent of almonds)
    warming lotion in
your palms

I'll return

to the word
as some people

turn to the forest.
words

(in the beginning)
made

(of true light)
words (dwelling among us)

begotten:
sun filtered through

a canopy of fir
or

needles shed
from a great tree.

I want to hold: light
(in fullness)

and the word for "light"
(the word was made!)

lines, angles,
curves

the shapes
(turning around)

(the darkness)
ink makes on paper

(all things were made)
(ascending, descending)

perhaps a word
(full of grace and truth)

perhaps a world
(full of grace and truth)

Part Three
Open Sesame

The Magician's Mother

Other moms plopped their children in a playpen or in front of the TV for at least a little while each day, but hers wouldn't have it. *Highly curious*, the doctor said. *Needs lots of mental stimulation.* Well what was she, a woman of average intelligence, of limited imagination, to do? Few toys enchanted him, and besides, his playthings were always vanishing. The magician's mother grieved over his first words—*open sesame*—and on the day he turned two, he made his cherry-wood rocking horse disappear right in front of her. Startled, sad to lose the treasured heirloom, she realized then he would never grow out of his eccentricities. Days passed, and like all moms, she'd gaze at her son sleeping peacefully in his crib, sun through the curtained window enhancing the talcum scent she knew would soon be memory. One exhausted afternoon, as she marveled at this child who was so incredibly demanding, he jumped up to touch her face with a threadbare rattle toy he held like a magic wand. *Mommy*—he'd leaned in close—*What's this?*—and laughed as his chubby fingers pulled a glistening nickel out of her ear.

What Rises, What Wanes

Daughter knows the alive
of batter
           of dough
pleases herself
in sift-measure-mix

           quickens as the griddle
crackles, hot grease spattering
low-riding
Levis. Pouring
and flipping

flipping and stacking
           she feeds
           her family with a vigor
           lacking at her own plate
—caught in the orbit

           of close observation
forking curves
in pancakes
           carving crescent
moons to thinnest.

Sundays she'll accept
the bread whole
           wafer thin
           as onionskin—
flesh

           transformed
  living
           in her bones
or full moon
      rising in her throat.

Baton

Flo—just turned seven—held up the sequined majorette outfit, tasseled baton, told her parents they'd have no regrets. Every day she practiced, feeling her talent glisten like a sunlit wishing pond, that sharp sparkle of carp and nickels. Summer of her twelfth year, adolescence blessed her: abundant breasts. Hair dark and thick. But follicles sent out runners like blackberry—sprouting from chest, stomach, chin. Upper lip. No callbacks from the drill team that fall. But when Uncle Sid, a carnival man, lost his honeymooning sword swallowers to divorce, things changed for Flo, starting with her name—Sid suggesting Esau's Sister, Flo's mom forbidding it on grounds of sacrilege. She settled on Monkey Girl, a long brown braid down her back doubling as a tail. Minnie the Tarot Reader groomed her daily, shampooing and braiding, gently untangling sideburns and beard with a comb tiny as the one used by the Living Doll. A giant banner wooed sugar-dizzy crowds: "For Just a Nickel See the World's Wild, Weird, Wonderful." Flo danced solo in a pink spangled leotard—proudly bending and arching her bristly back. Twirled her glittered baton, ate a lot of bananas. Only Fish Boy's lines were longer, the barker failing to disclose in his spiel that Fish was a mere half-inch of protoplasm pickled in a jar. Questioned in old age—how it felt to be exploited, a spectacle, Flo said only that her sister Sal was a beauty, a belle, not one misplaced hair, told how Sal cinched herself into girdle and high heels, waited tables at the Lodge, how Daddy's friends, the minister, the grammar-school principal, tipped well with quarters and dimes, her soft girl-ass bruised some nights from all the pinching.

Cornucopia

Boys in the field, gold as leaves
tough as pumpkins, do their
insides rattle like gourds

when helmets clack
when they fling
their trunks into stuffing-pocked

tackling dummies, do their insides rattle
like ours?
Whistles in the field, white

padded pants. Scent of fresh
mow, grunts
and bone-knocking booms

passing through chain link
while we ploink
and plink

in poly tennis dresses
gazelles alongside
goats, battle-ready.

First Friday match, first home game
and dance—gold leaves, shadowed
restless, grass stains

heart-soaked and permanent.
Whispers in the field,
young September

chilling the air with loss.
Maneuvering the angled sun's
pigskin, cat-gut chaos

we all gasp the same
rubber-sweating
chimney-smoked air

glance sidelong
wipe lip-clung sweat with forearms
toned and tanned.

Broken cleats
scuffed tennis shoes
summer slipping

through a funnel
into fields of Indian corn
bales of hay.

Kitchen

Your job is small and you do it well—
stir the pan of thickening gravy.
Mom orchestrates the meal, dodges hot oil
sputtering from the fry pan, drops giblets
into a paper sack heavy with flour
and Lawry's seasoned salt. She shakes it
for even coating, with tongs drops pieces
into the skillet. She does this after frying
the wings and legs and thighs and breasts,
because giblets don't take long.
The family will claim for themselves
all but the heart,
this is for her, crisp and savory,
a taste acquired in childhood
for what won't be missed,
for what settles in the palm's crease—
tablespoon of flour,
pinch of salt, celery seed.

Eskimo Pie

An August day on the way home from camping—me, Mom, Daddy, Jimmy—turning into the parking lot of a small grocery, our gold pickup smelling of ashes and hot Naugahyde and coffee, and it stung when my thighs unstuck from the seat. Daddy went in while we waited outside in the faint breeze and he brought back Eskimo Pies. I bit in deep to force the cold against my teeth and gums. The taste wasn't right and I frowned at the ice-cream beads forming underneath the two chocolate bumps where the stick came out, watched white droplets hit pavement and part of me wanted to throw it down, and I hated that I hated that he'd made a special stop on that scorching day, when I didn't know what I wanted but even so licked every last bit of the wooden stick until no chocolate remained and all I tasted was wood, and my tongue got scratched trying to make sure there was nothing sweet left on that stick. I gnawed on it a couple times too, sinking my teeth down into the flexible wood just like I'd always done, even before those stones of discontent slingshot me into adolescence, before I knew the restlessness of not knowing what I wanted, but knowing it wasn't Eskimo Pies.

Charm

Automatic doors seal shut, the air artificial and cool. Thick with the smell of a deep fat fryer, fresh butchered meat, bananas just out of cold storage. Mom gets a cart. You linger in this alcove of news racks and gumball machines, one filled with Chiclets, one with jawbreakers big as golf balls, and this one, the one that dazzles you, its display card alive with trinkets and plastic charms.... You align your dime into its special slot. Crank the metal handle. The mound of treasure shifts, a small upheaval, and you hear the plastic capsule sliding down the chute. Will it be a tiny bird whistle—yellow, orange, or baby blue—that when filled halfway with water and blown will chirp and warble? Or the salmon-pink Cupid with his sideways glance, bow drawn back, one leg flexed behind him? These would please you, held tightly in your hand or worn on a chain, but the miniature magnifying glass—something small that lets you see things even smaller, this is what you want, what you need and you already see yourself sliding it in and out of its little red sheath.

After Sunday School

Me, a pocketful of Swedish Fish
eyeing your Neccos

orderly row of Easter pastels
bound in their wax-paper shell.

I eat my fish
one after another

delighting in the gaudy
coat-of-many-colors

red, green, yellow jelly
stuck to the crowns of my teeth.

So you think Jesus
could turn two of these

into a feast
for the multitudes?

You ignore me, slowly
peel open one end of your Neccos

careful not to tear
with a press of forefinger

clasp of thumb
extract a powder-white wafer

suck on just that one
          all the way home.

Church Camp-out, 1978

Summer hearts buzz like sapphire dragonflies,
eight of us squeezed in the back of Pastor Dean's pickup
—fluorescent bikinis, faded cutoffs, the peculiar

pheromone of lake breeze, sweat, Sea & Ski
—my right thigh touching Ron Mayer's left and on Chris's
transistor radio, "Magic Man" by Heart,

that screech-and-pulse anthem to small-town adolescence.
At the beach, through dime store sunglasses,
I watch lanky boys, athletic girls, dive

from the rickety dock. Surrounded by splashes
and screams, Ron puts his arm around Ruth,
offers up his bright orange beach towel,

drapes it around her like a coronation cape.
Ruth—tall, tanned, starlight blonde—has the flush
of something freshly plucked, more than just sun

on her skin, though exactly *what*, exactly *how*, remains elusive,
something not for me. At Sunday morning's
campfire service, pretending Ruth is not there,

I sit on the log behind Ron, study the back of his head,
brown curls blending into swirls of smoke and sunlight,
fire burning strong, cedar logs crackling. We sing,

Pastor accompanying on guitar, each of my breaths
drawing into me the glories of God, his pines, his sky,
the magic words of each refrain

threading my voice to some vibrant fabric both holy
and earthly, suspending me
in an exquisite moment—my insides thrumming,

the rapid saw of crickets. When Ron turns to me,
whispers "This is Christ's body . . . ."
I open my palm to receive the bread. Briefly

our hands touch. Flames leap from my cheeks.
We close our eyes in prayer, sing "Morning Has Broken,"
my stomach tumbling, my spirit a popped ember flying.

The Zipper

Towering above other rides, neon latticework and steel teeth grinning through reek of vomit and hot grease, this was the ride I never went on, no matter how my brother begged, even the summer I knew he was going away.

It was a ride I didn't understand—too many different pulls of gravity— each double-seated cage cable-pulleyed around a suspended elongated arm, the arm meanwhile spinning on its own maniacal axis. Just as intimidating—the guys who pulled levers while cigarettes dangled from their smirks, ten-foot speakers belching Molly Hatchet, Judas Priest.

And years after my brother left, after I had gone too, that summer I was preoccupied with loving everything that wouldn't love me back, when I couldn't pick up the phone to call home for fear of missing calls that never came—that was the summer my mother started painting her empty house. Redecorating. Rearranging.

In a conversation years later my mother told me it was that empty-nest summer when, at the state fair held in the next town over, she rode the Zipper with a friend. At first I thought she was joking, but she said it was God's truth. While my stomach surged in retroactive worry, my heart fluttered with pride, envy even, though the image still disturbs me: her metal cage flipping over and over in the midst of stink and shrieks, until the spinning ceases, the machinery lurching her into the de-board zone—Butt-Rock-boy ushering her to safety, offering her his hand as she leaps to solid ground.

kiss

                    the first time
they left us alone you
                            painted your lips
                with Mercurochrome
drew on curved-up
        corners like the Joker's mouth
                        with the bottle's
glass wand.
                    I sat you down
on a bar stool you let me
                            cut your hair my hand
                clutched sheaf
                            after sheaf of it
                    thick and brown
it smelled like hay each
        creaking snip
                        of scissors launching
                                downward sails.
                    I blew away
the loose hair spun you
                    round you
said you liked it kissed
                        me sun's orange-
        red all salt and tin.

Part Four
Now You See It . . .

The Magician's Lover

He was really into sexual pyrotechnics. You didn't hear me complaining—who wouldn't jump at the chance to try every position in broad daylight, both of you completely invisible? Who wouldn't be willing to do a little extra strengthening and toning so they could act out their doing-it-while-suspended-in-midair fantasy? Sure, he had a couple of odd habits like keeping the top hat on and chanting *abra… cadabra…* in an ear-piercing falsetto before the dam broke, but no deal breakers. Thing is, I started to love him. And he was clear from the very start about that. With him, even a breakup was showbiz—the night we said goodbye he wanted to try it in the Houdini tank, but I knew my limitations. Later I unwrapped the box he'd sent home with me: a dozen paper roses that, when I held them, turned into white doves and flew away.

Yellow

Wasps again. In this room,
three, five at a time
arrive by morning through some secret portal
hunting for a dead or sweet thing.
The gaps and vents, I seal them shut
and still the morning brings
the frantic buzzing, heavy and confused
behind the blind.

* * *

In one dream they are benevolent,
here to devour the excess and rot—
piling paper, stinking fruit,
tainted meat.

* * *

Back! Back to your house of mud and spit
—your antennae with the twitch of wayward legs—
they've misinformed you. Leave here,
scavenge the abundance outside, ripe plums
fallen beneath the tree, orange meat busting
out of purple skins.

* * *

In another dream
I am a giant lily,
they a thousand honeybees . . .

* * *

I cannot keep them out.
Look into their black-bulb eyes,
recoil, repulsed.
Sickened by my own house,
waking to the fierce face
of something I cannot love.

I cannot keep them out,
the words "thorax,"

"exoskeleton," "grub."
"Infestation,"
"extermination."

* * *

And what if it's too late—
if I wake to the sound of crawling,
look up to a ceiling covered solid,
workers waiting for their queen,
her command to take flight
toward me—tiny black
and yellow swords.
What escape for me
when they swarm my spackled
airtight room,
even the windows painted shut.

None of These Belonging

You never imagined yourself thirty-eight
looking down at stone—

grave of the friend you met in junior high,
not best friends but friends over time—

she your companion in singleness
as your school-days circle

celebrated weddings and births.
You could use her by your side these days,

each hour you diverge
from the common dream.

Kitty-corner, two rows up
they've just buried the boy

who took you to the ninth-grade dance
—drove himself into a tree,

final tick of a heart
worked thin by a miscarried

daughter, a strayed wife.
Spring breeze rustles

green-eyed dogwood blossoms,
starts a plastic pinwheel twirling

over the plot of an unnamed baby.
A yellow tulip blooms large as an apple,

petals opened fully
flashing stigma, stamen—

your impulse to avert your eyes
from its brilliant center,

so exclamatory
        so exposed.

Tent, Two A.M.

Scent of air mattress, canvas
and pine should lull me
but instead I'm hemmed in
unsound, surrounded by starkness,
a hollow hum in my chest
off-key and dark, mind turning
to getaway, the car parked close by.
I unzip the door, feel smothered
by the immensity of night
pace a while outside then climb back in
panicked moth flapping above me
caught somewhere
between rain fly and tent. *Breathe.*
Find the flashlight. Turn to chapter three
of your paperback mystery.
The moth will stop its agitation,
an owl begin its otherworldly hoo-hooing.
The detective will make her town safe. Eventually.

Snow Day

Snowman believed in taking one day at a time.
He had just lost an eye.

Which was a 1978 penny.
The snow-woman across the street thought he was winking

and she winked back. But Snowman missed it
because his peripheral vision was now very bad.

On the bright side, everything smells sweet
when your nose is a carrot.

Even when one of your eyes
has just slid down your face because a crow

has been pecking at that nose and disturbed
your very shallow eye socket.

(Snowman's remaining eye was a silver dollar
which made him look like he was wearing a monocle.)

The crow eventually gave up and left the nose intact.
Thank goodness for a firmly planted proboscis!

Snowman added In God We Trust to his list of aphorisms.
The snow-woman wore a red Fendi scarf, which the crow coveted.

By noon the crow's nest was lined with couture.
Snowman felt sad that the snow-woman now

had nothing to keep her neck warm and he rejoiced
when the sun came out.

Snowman's silver-dollar eye stayed put
even as his body thinned, pinholes

forming with each tiny drip-drop falling from the branches above him.
His vision became obscured by floaters shaped like Eisenhower's head.

He became delirious and dreamed
that the snow-woman had turned into Carmen Miranda.

The fruit on her head grew wings and caused a commotion.
In his last lucid moment Snowman thought

tomorrow I will tell the snow-woman about those
flying papayas. I think she'll get a kick out of that.

Bigfoot Car Wash

It's easy to miss on this four-lane strip,
overshadowed by its neighbors—girlie
bar to the north, Discount Gun to the south.
Defunct neon, no triangle streamers
or inflatable sasquatch to lure you in.
The faded sign is painted milk-glass green
and pale pink and long ago stopped spinning
though you can see the namesake line-drawn foot
a traffic light down. You make your purchase,
the Deluxe, shift to neutral. Conveyed through
short-lived storms, sounds of troubled autumn seas
you fret, want to build a website or start
a Facebook group for Bigfoot, protect it
from encroachers: Starbucks, invasive weeds.

Endangered

Now, please turn your attention to a vanishing habitat—two-lane highways that taper into Main Streets, family-owned "variety" stores, drive-ins with names like Coop 'n' Scoop and Biff's. In such environs the vigilant may find the rare but easy-to-identify *Fiberglassis giantessus*, commonly known as Uniroyal Gal. Towering over *Homo sapiens* at heights up to fifteen feet, she has facial features bearing an uncanny likeness to the late Jackie Onassis and tends to live alone with few social interactions. The typical Gal adorns herself in a skirt, midthigh to mini, and a short-sleeved sweater (see *Chanel*) that emphasizes her well-developed upper torso, though variations in attire can be found in warmer climes. It is common for an individual of this species to gravitate toward industrial quarters, where she may be seen standing guard over gas pumps and roadside motels. Look for a tire or sandwich platter brandished in her upraised fist.

Letter from Zelda

My darling Scott, I feel so exploded
I can barely write, like a gourd
not knowing the hand that shakes me,

my mind a million seeds.
But weren't we once grand—a Ferris
wheel in Paris, spinning ourselves silly.

I never loved you more than when you bent
over your desk, pen gouging paper,
never hated you more—

your pen always blackening,
always my paper white as dogwood.
And though you cried,

your relief heavied the air when you left me
in this room—where everything is cream-colored
rest—no silver shoes, dance floors, gin, or us.

I've planted a sunflower seed—I give it water
from the pitcher on my bed stand.
One day its yellow head will be as full as mine.

We Have All Entered a Nesting Phase

Every day a bird
perches on a tree
outside your cordless bladeless room.

Its beak opens and closes but never a sound.
It was you in the neighborhood who rescued
rodents from the cat, wrapped anything maimed

in something warm.
Stay, stay, stay, stay—
lately friends are hard to hold on to.

Your nights bleached still,
clicks and squeaks of med nurses' carts
the sound of summer crickets.

They've hidden your sadness
in a sock drawer.
A giant blue pill sits on the windowsill, sings.

Disappearing

When the magician made me disappear, I felt a lurch in my stomach, a zap in my skull. He hadn't explained fully—something to do with condensing matter and forcing a square peg into the sphere of fourth dimension. I imploded into a brooding mass, feeling liquid, dispersed, unaware of a center. Sound was the muffled din heard from within a car on the ferry ride across the bay, and the room became a revolving Cubist mural. I felt things floating through me and thought *This is the translucent life of amoebae or squid, this is what it is to be the Holy Ghost.* When the magician brought me back, I thought *This is the shimmer of life between transparent and opaque* and took my bow.

Refusal

Sad, this blade of grass, the way the wind doubles it over. The beetle world below burdened too. It's always been about decay, but there had been a kind of gallows humor. Now something's off-kilter, more than the usual workaday ennui (this endless cycle, this samsara...). Toward earth's core earthworms tunnel down and linger. Mycelia cease their creeping. Mushrooms no longer multiply, won't release their spores, and greenbottle flies buzz away from the corpse. If you listen closely—carried on the sour breeze—the microcosm's heavy sigh.

Disquiet

I walk the dark past
cinnamon shop windows

holding incense, magic boxes
—turn that late hour

even farther
from home. Salamanders

asleep in their glass.
Moonlight in jars

tightly shut. I could lose my way
wanting.

Part Five
Voilà!

Groundhog Turning Poet

Burrow back down.
Your work in the dark is not done.

Because the autumn was nothing
but gathering

and digging
you've still got seeds

and roots to gnaw and swallow.
What's the hurry?

You hibernators.
So lucky.

Months of no distractions from the moon.
The strange dreams of slowed

metabolism, knowing when
to look at shadows.

Treasure

Somewhere there's a key, lost
in the rubble of a cobwebbed garage

or wedged in the corner of a moss-covered shed.
Who will find it, hold it in her hand,

rub away the rust and muck?
What you hope for—not treasure in a padlocked box

but another unlocking:
rush of strawberry air, hint of hay

that years ago kept you awake;
climbing down the fire ladder, over the gate,

meeting your best friend in moonlit pasture
to ride your father's horses bareback—remember

how you'd turn toward home when you heard the horn
of the morning's first ferry crossing the bay?

Trying to Get Across

The Evergreen Point Floating Bridge (officially the Governor Albert D. Rosellini Bridge) connects Seattle and Medina, Washington.

Condensation on my windshield, driving toward a hidden sun.

Morning traffic stalls.

Variations of silver and grey: wet concrete, mist, the bridge's truss.

A gull on the cobra-head fixture of the roadway light.

Steel, this dull inside my head.

Can I wait it into opalescence.

Some might call it paradox, wheels spinning every day across a
   bridge that floats.

A double suspension, deliberate ungrounding.

What's beneath us in its own stasis:

No Loch Ness monster but a sturgeon, longer than any man, older
   than a hundred years.

Oblivious to the red brake lights beading the bridge deck above it.

A forecast of clouds, rain, and we wait.

For everything to start its churning.

Lake's surface choppy, iridescent.

The gull ruffling its wings.

Huntress

Get lost in the woods,
the nighttime timbre.

Listen for mating calls
of the phoneme—

dissonant chittering,
glottal stops.

With a flashlight, watch
for ascenders

reaching out
from stone-cover, for

*g*s, *y*s, *j*s, *p*s, and *q*s
hanging from trees

like possums.
Pluck them

from what they cling to,
stuff them

kicking and screaming
into your knapsack,

the unruly bunch strapped
to your back. Walk fast.

Feel the ire
of poke and paw,

the jab of *k* in your
spine, sharp kicks

of *v*s and *x*s.
Back in your study

release them,
watch their acrobatic

leaps—serifs hook
and bodies tumble—

watch them arrange
and rearrange

in alphabetic ecstasy,
in combinations

disallowed,
in meanings

more or less.

Metronome Ticking

Man Ray is listening for light
—André Breton

pose it
     shadow it

picture it (backlit

incandescent
    dissent)

plastic hand holding
       imagine

       what aperture

 this ordinary junk
      drawn eye

     to catch
a pair of

     disembodied
lips
     floating
       on a
cloud

an unrepressed

     double under
over-
     exposure

silver shrouded

     nitrate ghost

the metronome

       the plaster
       bust   the fist

     the hand the
mannequin dealt

Reappearing

During intermission, the magician took me aside, showed me to a room he'd recently discovered behind a false wall, turned on the light, and said, *Look at this!* as if I would grasp the significance. My blank look prompted him to explain the white rabbits hopping among coins and dollar bills, paper bouquets, and various fake fruits. *When you're first learning the disappearing act*, he said, *you make mistakes. Very common. Turns out it's all a matter of voice—like training a dog—but even so, objects can be stubborn, refuse to return to their vanishing points. Most upsetting to someone who's entrusted you with an heirloom watch or brooch. Imagine my pleasure at recovering such losses!* Now it all made sense—the mound of Boston Red Sox caps, unmatched shoes, sets of keys. And in that cobwebbed corner, the marriage certificate, the gold band, the thin flask of shame.

A Quiet

A quiet poem when I want to shout
about the whole depraved, relentless
brilliant band of humans I belong to.

Turn to goodness,
second chances. How papyrus
just restored tells of Judas—

not the villain but
the Lord's most trusted friend,
how only his steady love

could be counted on to do
the hardest thing. Let me think
inside out, upside

down, and sideways, remember
I'm one of the lucky who saw her brother
come home from war, gets to love him

as if before me is a whole other lifetime.
If there's a patron saint of second chances
I surely wear her medallion, and may I add

stupid and *careless* to the list I opened
up with—what it takes to drive
through two-lane counties after nights without sleep,

to nod yourself awake, find your car
across the line. Oh, split-second
chances, all I don't deserve, the judgments I hand out.

A jealous streak to rival Joseph's brothers
who betrayed him, announced him dead.
We know the rest—the dreams, Pharaoh, the rise

to greatness. But most extraordinary—when Joseph
sent for the eleven he hadn't seen since childhood,
served them a feast, revealed himself to their astonished

hearts, that room filled
with weeping men.
That room

filled with weeping.

What Ignites

Only the sound of your teeth as they snick
the nutmeat of one salted pistachio
after another. Weary of August's
soft-fleshed fruit, you long for cold's sharp claw to

scratch you awake. Anticipate harvest's
fresh-gleaned grain, as if swallowing kernel,
husk, might grow something new inside (such grand
thoughts accumulate when leaves start to curl).

You'll watch pumpkins on the fence—faces blend
into low-slanting sun, mouths carved open—
frozen midword. Offer up horse chestnuts,
letters from ghosts, feathers of sin to candle-

flame tongues. Praise what ignites, dissipates. Plant
seeds of pomegranate in mind's blank dusk.

Restoration

—for C & J

Tell me again of your visit to the south, your first
encounter with a cottonmouth—its head full of poison
sliced clean by the blade of a cowman's
shovel, how he put on leather work gloves
grabbed the snake's body and pitched it
high over the barbed wire fence—
the head remaining, olive-colored scales
catching light from the sun, creating an illusion
of shimmering life.

How that night the half-moon climbed slowly up
the clear August sky. How you lay alone
in your freshly laundered guestroom bed
the window propped open—
listening to the scurry and scratch
of night animals, pond frogs chirping—
and breathed in the night's cool air, longing
for all that had ever been severed from you.

Tell me again of the next morning, when you woke early
made coffee, wandered out to the place of yesterday's trouble
how you stared in disbelief when you found the snake's mottled body
aligned perfectly behind its sunbaked head. How this turned your mind
to the lady-sawed-in-half stage act, the myth of Osiris, the resurrection
stories of your own withered faith.

How you stood there awhile
as dawn performed its own transformations.

Sculptor

Then, what do you love, extraordinary stranger?
I love the clouds...the clouds that pass...up there...
up there...the wonderful clouds!
    —*Charles Baudelaire*

He drove around in his beat-up Pinto all day offering clouds to people, but they mostly refused, saying things like "Clouds? Don't we got enough of them, you loony old man?" Mrs. Eastman the science teacher said, "Of course they couldn't *really* be clouds, now could they, class? After all, did you ever see it *raining* in Cloud Man's car?" A group of us waited for him to show every Friday out by the junior high baseball diamond. He'd bring John long cirrus strands to wrap around his neck like a feather boa. Heidi preferred dark and brooding thunderclouds, which she herded up to her attic bedroom to hover over her collection of Gothic novels. I could tell when Cloud Man had gone the extra mile to bring my favorites—the ones shaped like silhouettes of TV stars. He'd pull up grinning and yell, "Got ya some good ones, kid!" One March day I'll never forget, he brought three of them—cumulus, well hewn, so big he had to bungee the hatchback closed. I skipped all the way home hugging my cloud bouquet: Ernest Borgnine, Cher, and Ricardo Montalban.

Company Party

Some know-it-all at this party was debunking the childhood
chanting game "Light as a Feather, Stiff as a Board"
played late at night in candle-lit basements

or bedrooms by girls in pajamas ready to be amazed
and spooked. He was saying it merely proves
the power of suggestion and the constancy

of physics, but as with all attempts to intertwine
science with the supernatural, I wasn't buying
and said so, and around me heads nodded in assent.

Look, I said to him, *I experienced it myself,*
four friends kneeling around me, eight
bony fingers slid beneath me

—when we started whispering "light as a feather,
stiff as a board," I felt a force from underneath, and when
we started saying it louder and louder I rose steadily

up, I was engaged with the air!—I hadn't realized
I was so passionate about this—*We had harnessed*
some sort of power! By now a group of co-workers

had gathered around me—we clinked glasses
and started chanting *Light as a feather, stiff as a board,*
light as a feather, stiff as a board,

and that's when the CEO started floating up to the chandelier,
followed by the president and vice-president, and before long
the whole ceiling was covered with middle managers.

Those of us still standing were thinking
about another drink
and the know-it-all was jabbing his finger

in our eyes, saying something about static
electricity and magnetic poles.
While we ignored him, someone asked

the DJ to play "Stayin' Alive" and we danced
under the glittering disco ball, mesmerized
by the strange shadows it cast.

About the Author

Marjorie Manwaring lives in Seattle, where she is a freelance writer/ editor, co-editor of the online poetry and art journal the *DMQ Review*, and editorial board member for Floating Bridge Press. Her poems have appeared in a variety of journals and anthologies, including *5 AM, Sentence,* and *A Face to Meet the Faces: An Anthology of Contemporary Persona Poetry*, and her poems have been featured on National Public Radio affiliate KUOW. Marjorie holds an MFA in Creative Writing and Literature from the Bennington College Writing Seminars and is the author of two chapbooks, *What to Make of a Diminished Thing* (Dancing Girl Press) and *Magic Word* (Pudding House Publications); this is her first full-length collection.